SCIENCE WITH MAGNETS

Helen Edom

Designed by Radhi Parekh and Diane Thistlethwaite
Illustrated by Simone Abel

Consultants: Joan and Maurice Martin

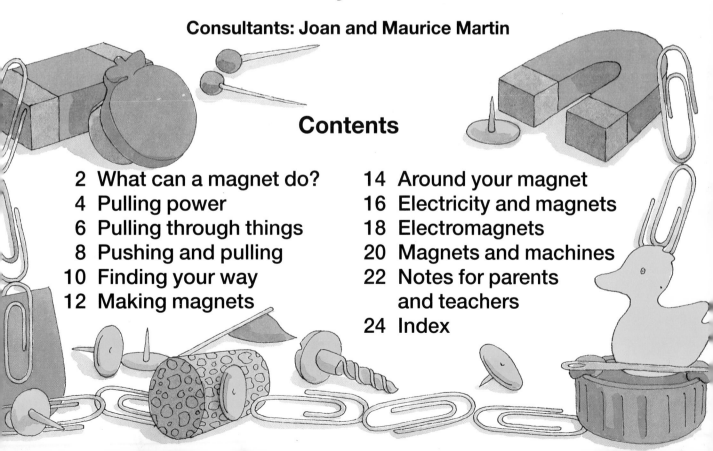

Contents

What can a magnet do?

The experiments and games in this book will help you find out what magnets can do. You can use any magnet for most of the activities but you will need bar magnets for some of them.

Horseshoe magnet

Bar magnet

Button magnet

Sticking test

Magnets stick to some things but not to others. Find different things to test with your magnet.

Here are some things you can try. Make a chart to show what happens with each one.

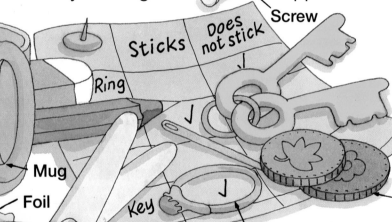

Screw

Sticks | Does not stick

Ring

Mug

Foil

Key

Jewelry

Coins

Try this test with different magnets. See if the same things stick.

Bottle top

Look at the things that stick to the magnet. Are they all metal?

Look at the things that do not stick. Are any of them metal?

Magnets and metals

Everything that sticks to a magnet is made of metal. Only some metals such as iron, steel and nickel stick to magnets. Other metals such as aluminum do not stick at all.

Useful magnets

Look around your home to see if you can find magnets being used.

Magnet **Steel plate**

Magnets keep some cupboards closed.

Magnetic letters can spell words on metal doors.

Sorting cans

Cans are usually made of aluminum or steel. Try a magnet out on lots of different ones. The ones that do not stick are aluminum.

Old cans are melted so their metal may be used again. Magnets are used to sort the cans so aluminum ones can be melted separately.

*Cellophane tape

Matching socks game

Use the sticking power of your magnet to make a game.

You need: 2 magnets, thread, paper, paints or crayons, sticky tape*, scissors, paper-clips, large box.

Cut the paper into sock shapes. Color them in twos so they look like different pairs. Put a paperclip on each one.

Throw the socks into the box. Tape a thread to each magnet. Taking turns with a friend, dip a magnet into the box and pull out a sock.

See who can get the most pairs.

Pulling power

Magnets can pull, or attract, some metal things towards them.

Pulling test

See how far your magnet can pull a pin.

Put a ruler flat on a table.

▲
Place a pin at zero (0) on the ruler.

Put the magnet four inches away. Push it slowly towards the pin. Wait for a few seconds at each mark.

When the pin jumps to the magnet, look at the number beside the magnet. This shows how far the pin has jumped.

▼

This magnet pulls the pin about 1½ inches.

Using pulling power

Workers who build things out of steel can get tiny splinters of steel in their eyes. Doctors use a special magnet to pull the splinters out.

Magnet

Try the same test with as many magnets as you can. See which one can pull the pin furthest.

CHAMP

You could write down your results on a chart like this.

Magnet used	Pulls pin
My magnet	1½ in
Alfie's magnet	¾ in
Fridge magnet	1 in

— Chart

Force

Magnets make things move with an invisible pull. This is called magnetic force.

Try pulling a pin off a magnet. Feel the magnetic force pulling back. You have to pull more strongly than the magnet.

Gravity

The Earth tries to pull everything down towards its centre. This pull is called the force of gravity. You have to pull against it when you lift things up.

Pulling upward

Hold the ruler up against the edge of a table so zero is level with the table-top. Put a pin at zero.

Sticky tape helps to keep the ruler upright.

Slide your strongest magnet slowly down the ruler until the pin jumps up. Stop and look at the number beside the magnet.

The magnet cannot pull the pin as far as before. This is because another kind of force is trying to pull the pin down. This is the force of gravity (see above right).

Flying butterfly

Cut a butterfly shape out of some tissue. Slide a paperclip on to it.

Tie one end of a thread to the clip. Tape the other end to a table.

See if you can make the butterfly fly without letting your magnet touch the clip.

The force of gravity tries to pull the clip down.

Pulling through things

Try these experiments to see if you can stop a magnet working.

Blocking test

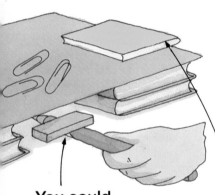

Rest a sheet of paper across two piles of books. Put paperclips on top.

You could tape the magnet on to a pencil.

Rest more books on top to keep the paper still.

Hold a magnet underneath. Can you make it move the clips?

The magnet works through the paper. See if it can work through other things.

Plastic

Cardboard

Here are some you could try.

Cloth

Foil

Sticky metal

Find a metal lid that sticks to a magnet. Put a paperclip on top. See if the magnet can move the clip from under the lid.

You could use a baking tray instead.

The paperclip is hard to move or may not move at all. This is because the iron or steel in the lid traps the magnet's force.

Keepers

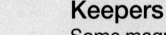

Some magnets are sold with a piece of iron on them, called a keeper.

Keeper on a horse-shoe magnet.

The keeper stops the magnet attracting things when it is not being used.

Bar magnets are stored in pairs with two keepers.

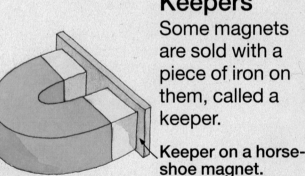

6

Fun with water

Rest the tray across two piles of magazines. Pour water inside. Push a pin into each cork and put it in the water.

You could pin on paper sails to make the corks look like boats.

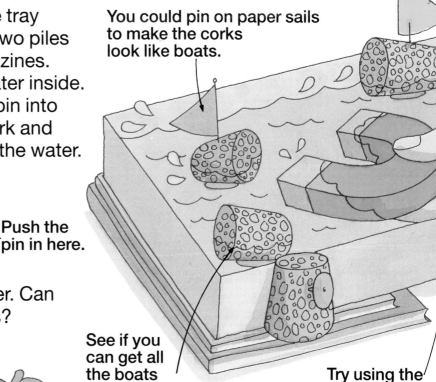

Push the pin in here.

Hold the magnet underwater. Can you make it move the corks?

See if you can get all the boats in one corner.

Try using the magnet under the tray as well.

Magnetic holders

Because magnets can work through paper and paint, they can be used to hold up notices on a refrigerator's metal door.

Magnetic puzzle

Put a sheet of paper and a nail on a table. How can you use your magnet to pick up the paper? The experiments on this page should give you a clue.

If you get stuck, turn to the answer on page 24.

Pushing and pulling

These experiments will help you find out more about a magnet's force.

Where is a magnet strongest?

Put a magnet into a box of pins. Lift it out carefully. Where are there most pins? Try this experiment with all sorts of magnets.

A bar shape has most pins at the ends.

A horseshoe magnet has lots of pins at both ends.

This round magnet is strongest on each flat side.

Every magnet has two strong places. These are called poles. They are at opposite ends.

About poles

Both poles pick up pins in the same way. Try this experiment to see if the poles are the same in other ways.

1. Put two bar magnets eight inches apart, so the ends face each other. Push one towards the other. Watch what happens.

▼

Do not hold this one.

Watch how this magnet moves.

◀ 2. Tape colored paper on to the poles (ends) that stick. Use two different colors.

3. Turn both magnets round. Do the other poles also stick? Mark them so each magnet has its poles in different ◀ colors, as shown.

8

4. Now try to push two of the same-colored poles together. Can you feel them pushing back?

Each magnet has two sorts of pole. One is called north, the other south*. Poles of the same kind push each other away but different poles pull towards each other.

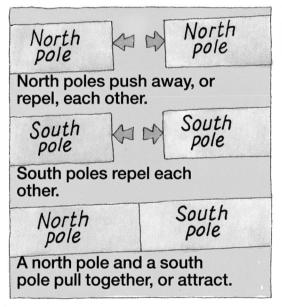

North pole ◄ ►	North pole
North poles push away, or repel, each other.	
South pole ◄ ►	South pole
South poles repel each other.	
North pole	South pole
A north pole and a south pole pull together, or attract.	

Try putting different shaped magnets together. Can you find which poles are the same?

*You can find out more about these on pages 10 and 11.

Pushing game

Tape one magnet on to a toy car. Use one pole of another magnet to push the car along.

How fast can you make the car go?

Floating magnets

Use the marked magnets for this trick. First cut some thin strips of sticky tape.

Put a pencil on one magnet. Put the other magnet on top so the same colors are together. ► Join the magnets with tape.

Keep the tape loose like this.

Now take the pencil away. The top magnet floats above the bottom magnet.

Try pressing this magnet.

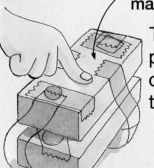

The same-colored poles try to push each other away. This keeps the magnet in the air.

9

Finding your way

Magnets help sailors, explorers and hikers to find their way. Here you can find out how.

Pointing magnet

Tape a bar magnet into a plastic pot. Float the pot in a bowl of water. Let the pot settle.

Mark the bowl opposite the two ends of the magnet.

Use a felt-tip pen for the marks.

Turn the pot, then let go. What happens?

The magnet turns back to face the same way.

A magnet always turns to point the same way, if it can swing easily. Its north pole (see page 9) points north. Its south pole points south.

Finding north

The sun always rises in the east and sets in the west. If you get up early and face the sun, north is on your left.

Never look straight at the sun. It can hurt your eyes badly.

Mark the north end of the magnet with a blob of plasticine* or paint.

Make a compass

Card

Cut a circle of cardboard to fit in the pot. Mark east, west, north and south.

Just use the first letters.

When the compass is finished it always shows the right directions.

Put the card in the pot so 'N' is over the north end of the magnet. Then all the arrows will point the right way.

10

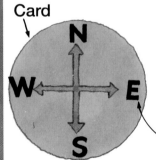

*Plastic modeling cl[...]

Chinese inventors

The Chinese invented the first compasses. This one had a magnet inside the turtle shape.

The magnet made the turtle turn so its head pointed north.

How a hiker's compass works

A hiker's compass has a magnetic needle. It always points north.

The needle stays still while the card turns.

To find other directions, the hiker turns a card beneath. When N (north) is under the needle all the arrows point the right way.

Another north pole

The north poles of all magnets point to one place. This place is called the Earth's magnetic north pole. It is in the icy, northern Arctic.

Explorers have found that compasses do not work at the Earth's north pole. The magnet inside just spins around.

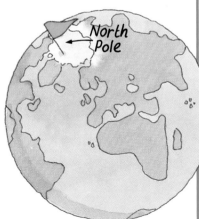

North Pole

Compass puzzle

Which way does this hiker have to go to get to the mountains?

Remember the hiker has to turn the compass so 'N' is under the needle.

Answer on page 24.

Making magnets

You can use one magnet to make another. Here are some ways to try this.

Hanging magnets

Hang a nail from the end of a magnet. Try hanging another nail on to the first one. Does it stick?

You can use pins instead of nails.

Magnet's north pole

◄ The first nail is a magnet while it is touching the big magnet. Like all magnets, the nail has two poles.

Nail's north pole

Now hang two nails side by side. Try pushing the pointed ends together. ▶

The ends have the same poles so they push each other away.

A lasting magnet

Stroke one pole of a magnet along a needle. Then lift the magnet away. Repeat 12 times.

The needle becomes a lasting magnet. See how many pins it can pick up.

Stroke the same way each time.

Inside a magnet

A magnet is made of many tiny parts called domains. Each one is like a mini-magnet. They all line up and point the same way.

Any metal that sticks to a magnet also has domains. These are jumbled up. A magnet can make them line up. Then the metal becomes a magnet.

Domains

Domains in an ordinary needle

Domains in a magnetized needle

Magnetic rock

A rock called magnetite is a natural magnet. It was first found at a place called Magnesia. All magnets get their name from this place.

Can you spoil a magnet?

Drop a magnetized needle on a table. Do this a few times. Then see if the needle can pick up pins.

What happens

The domains are shaken out of line so the needle stops being a magnet. Take care not to hit or drop your magnets in case they get spoiled in the same way.

Swimming ducks

You need:
2 needles,
magnet,
plastic
bottle tops,
plasticine,
paper,
scissors.

Magnetize two needles with your magnet. Stroke them both from the eye to the point.

Both needles will have the same poles at the same ends.

◀ Use plasticine to stick each one to a bottle top. Cut out duck shapes and stick them on top.

Stick one duck so its beak is over the needle's eye. Stick the other so its beak is over the point.

Float the bottle tops in water. The ducks seem to swim towards each other. ▼

These ends have different poles so they attract each other.

Around your magnet

Try these experiments so you can find out more about the forces around your magnet.

Magnetic field

Magnetic force works above and below a magnet as well as at its sides.

Magnet patterns

Put a magnet under some cardboard. Sprinkle iron filings on top. Tap it lightly. What happens?

Sprinkle the filings evenly.

The magnet pulls the filings into a pattern around it. This shows that a magnet's force works all round, although it is strongest at the poles.

Pattern made by a bar magnet.

Pattern made by a horseshoe magnet.

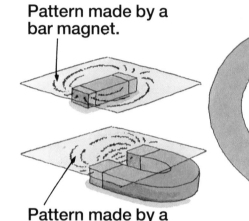

Using iron filings

Iron filings are tiny pieces of iron. Ask an adult to make some by filing an iron nail.

Chemistry sets often have iron filings in tubes like this.

Travelling needle

You need: needle, slice of cork, bar magnet, plasticine, bowl of water, sticky tape.

Magnetize a needle by stroking it with the south pole of a magnet. Stroke the needle 12 times from the eye to the point.

The point will have a north pole.

The space where a magnet's force works is called its magnetic field.

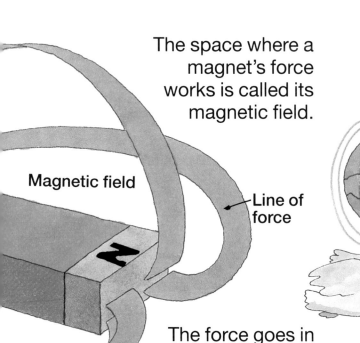

Magnetic field

Line of force

The force goes in lines which run from the north to the south pole of a magnet. These are called lines of force.

The Earth's magnetic field

The planet Earth behaves as if it has a huge magnet inside. It has a magnetic field like other magnets.

Some birds can feel the Earth's magnetic field. Scientists think that this helps them find their way when they fly. No one really knows how.

Push the needle through the cork. Float it in the water so the point is on top.

— Be careful with sharp things.

Stick plasticine under the cork so it floats upright.

Tape the magnet inside the bowl. Move the needle near to the magnet's north pole. Then let go.

The needle floats round to the south pole. It follows a line of force in the magnetic field.*

*Re-magnetize the needle if you want to try this again.

Tape the magnet well above the water.

Electricity and magnets

Electricity can act like a magnet. Here you can find out how.

What is electricity?

Electricity is caused by tiny invisible things called electrons. These move easily through metal. Their flow is called an electric current.

Danger

Only use batteries for experiments. Never use electricity from plugs and sockets. This is too strong and is dangerous.

Electrons flow along metal wires.

Electric surprise

You need: 4·5 volt battery, a 2 in piece of straw, needle, sticky tape, scissors, 60 in of plastic coated wire.

1. Ask an adult to help you cut off the plastic at each end of the wire. Tape one end on to a terminal on the battery. ▼

Terminal

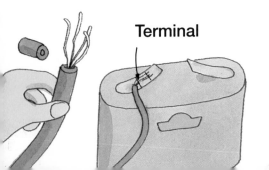

Trim the ends of the straw.

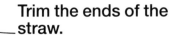

2. Wind the wire on to the straw ◄ to make a coil. Wind on three layers of wire.

Use tape to hold the turns together.

3. Tape the free end of the wire to the second terminal. Hold the needle lightly just inside the coil. What happens? ▼

When both terminals are joined, a current flows through the wire.

4. The needle is pulled inside ▶ the coil. This is because an electric current has a magnetic field. The coil makes the field strong enough to attract the needle.

This coil is called a solenoid.

Your battery will quickly run down if you leave the solenoid on for long. Switch it off by taking one wire off a terminal.

Railway signal

Use your solenoid to make a model signal.

Move the pin to make the signal balance.

Make sure the signal can swing.

You need: paper, straw, scissors, thread, needle, drawing pin, plasticine, solenoid.

◀ Stand the straw in some plasticine. Pin the signal to the top of the straw. Use plasticine to secure the solenoid beneath the needle.

Cut the paper into this signal shape. Thread the needle and sew it on to the thin end. ▼

The needle should hang just inside the solenoid.

Touch both wires to the terminals to switch the solenoid on.

Squeeze the plasticine to raise or lower the solenoid.

It pulls the needle down, raising the signal. ▶

Electromagnets

Some magnets use electricity to make them work. These are called electromagnets.

Making an electromagnet

You can turn the solenoid on page 16 into an electromagnet. Just put a long iron or steel nail inside the straw. Then tape both wires to the battery.
▼

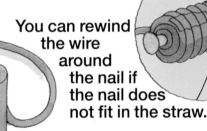

You can rewind the wire around the nail if the nail does not fit in the straw.

Now see if your ▶ electromagnet picks up the same things as other magnets.

Try pins, paperclips and nails.

Magnetic cranes

Some cranes use electromagnets to pick up iron and steel. These magnets are very strong.

The driver switches this magnet off to make the crane drop its load. ──────▶

Why the electromagnet works

The metal inside the solenoid strengthens its magnetic field. This makes a strong magnet.

Switching off

Now take one end of the wire away from the battery to stop the current. See if paperclips still stick. ▶

The electromagnet stops working because the magnetic field leaves the wire when the current stops flowing*.

*If the nail inside is still magnetic, turn to page 23 to find out why.

Making a toy crane

You can use an electro-magnet to make a crane.

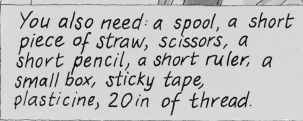

You also need: a spool, a short piece of straw, scissors, a short pencil, a short ruler, a small box, sticky tape, plasticine, 20 in of thread.

1. Tape the ruler inside the box, as shown. Stick the spool behind it with plasticine. Push the pencil into the spool, point downwards.

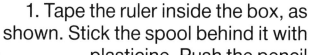

One end of a spool has a notch. This goes on top.

Add tape to keep the spool steady.

2. Tape the straw on to the ruler. Push the thread through the straw. Tie one end to the electromagnet. Tape the other end to the pencil, leaving a tail. ▼

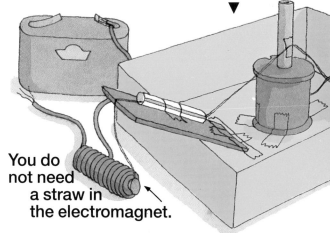

You do not need a straw in the electromagnet.

3. Put the battery inside the box. Tape both wires to the terminals when you want to pick up a load. Turn the pencil to wind the electromagnet up. ▼

Pull one wire off the terminal when you want to drop a load.

Push the tail into the notch to stop the thread unwinding.

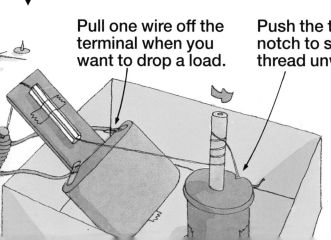

You could stick everything into a truck, instead of a box, to make a mobile crane.

Magnets and machines

Magnets help to make many electric machines work. Here you can find out about some of them.

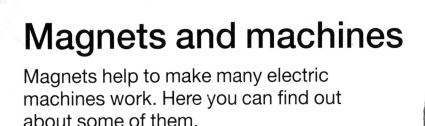

Magnet

Coil of wire spins.

Magnet

Making electricity

A machine called an electric generator is used to make electricity. The generator has a coil of wire with magnets around it.

Electric generator

This rod turns.

A rod turns the coil of wire in between the magnets. When the coil turns in the magnetic field, electricity flows through the wire.

An electric motor

An electric motor has a coil of wire and magnets like a generator but works the other way round. The coil is still until electricity flows into it from a battery. The flow of electricity in between the magnets makes the coil spin.

Axle

Rod

Here you can see how an electric motor turns the wheels in a toy car.

An electric motor in a toy car

Axle

Coil of wire

Magnets

The spinning coil makes this rod turn round and round.

The rod makes the wheels turn, so the car moves along.

Tape recorders

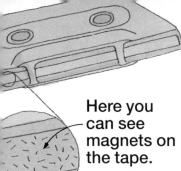

Here you can see magnets on the tape.

A tape is covered in tiny magnets. These are used to record sounds in a tape recorder.

When someone speaks into a microphone, it changes the sound into electrical signals.

Microphone

The signals go to an electromagnet. This arranges the magnets on the tape in a pattern to match the signals. ▶

The electromagnet is called a recording head.

Tape recorder

Signals go along this wire.

When you play the tape it moves past a different electromagnet, called a playback head. The pattern makes this head give off electrical signals. ▶

This pattern stays on the tape to record the sound.

Playback head

These are the same as the signals made when the sound was recorded. They go to a loudspeaker which uses them to make the sound again.

Loudspeaker ▼

See for yourself

Try wiping a magnet along an old tape that no one wants. Then play the tape.

Turn the reels with a pencil.

The tape will not work properly. This is because the magnet has destroyed the pattern that recorded the sound.

Notes for parents and teachers

These notes are intended to help answer any questions that arise from the activities on earlier pages.

Pulling power (pages 4-5)

A strong magnet can affect an object at a greater distance than a weaker one. It is said to have a stronger magnetic field (see page 14).

Gravity

All planets pull things towards their centre. This pull, or gravitational force, makes things feel heavy when you lift them. If it did not act, everything on the planet would become weightless and float around.

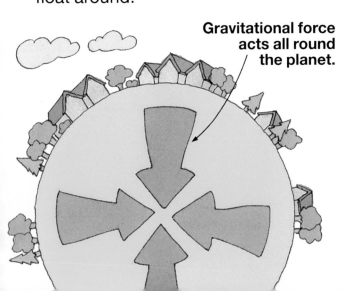

Gravitational force acts all round the planet.

Pulling through things (pages 6-7)

Magnetic force is almost unaffected by things a magnet does not attract. It works as well through a sheet of paper as it does through air. A thick wad of paper may seem to stop a magnet working. But this is simply because the depth of paper keeps objects out of the magnet's field. However, even a thin sheet of iron, steel or nickel does interfere with a magnet's field.

Keepers

Iron keepers trap the magnetic field so there are no free poles (see page 8) to attract other objects. This closed circuit helps to keep the field strong.

Direction of magnetic field

Pushing and pulling (pages 8-9)

Every type and shape of magnet has two kinds of pole; north and south. In every case, unlike poles attract; like ones repel each other.

Finding your way (pages 10-11)

The Earth's magnetic field (see page 15) acts as if it has a south pole in the Arctic. This attracts the north poles of all magnets. The place where they point is confusingly known as the magnetic north pole.

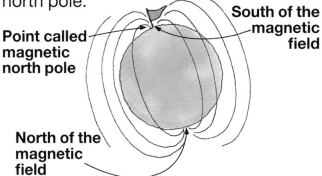

Point called magnetic north pole

South of the magnetic field

North of the magnetic field

Making magnets (pages 12-13)

Different magnetic metals have different qualities. Soft iron is easy to magnetize but also loses its magnetism easily. Steel is harder to magnetize but keeps its magnetism unless hammered or heated.

Electricity and magnets (pages 16-17)

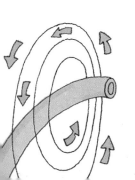

A current flowing in a wire produces a magnetic field in a pattern of concentric circles. A large current has a strong field.

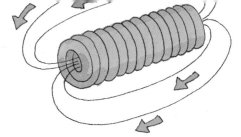

Coiling the wire into a solenoid increases the amount of current-carrying wire. It also creates a magnetic field like that of a bar magnet.

Wires to use

Plastic-coated wire works well and can be bought from any electrical shop. Glazed copper wire gives even better results but is more difficult to find.

Plastic-coated wire

Electromagnets (pages 18-19)

An iron or steel core strengthens the magnetic field of a solenoid. This makes a strong magnet. An electromagnet can be made even stronger by making more turns of the wire or increasing the current.

Copper wire

Core

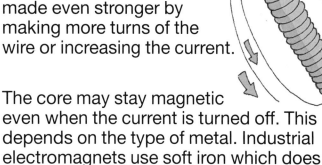

The core may stay magnetic even when the current is turned off. This depends on the type of metal. Industrial electromagnets use soft iron which does not stay magnetic (see above left).

Index

Answers to puzzles

Page 7 – Put the nail under the paper. Then put your magnet on top. The magnet sticks to the nail through the paper.

The paper is now squashed between the nail and the magnet so you can lift it up by raising the magnet.

Page 11 – The hiker has to go north to get to the mountains.

First published in 1990 by Usborne Publishing Ltd, Usborne House, 83-85 Saffron Hill, London, EC1N 8RT, England. Copyright © 1992, 1990 Usborne Publishing Ltd. This edition published in 1992.